GREAT SOCCER

BY JONATHAN AVISE

DEBATES

GREAT
SPORTS
DEBATES

SportsZone

An Imprint of Abdo Publishing | abdopublishing.com

ABDOPUBLISHING.COM

Published by Abdo Publishing, a division of ABDO, PO Box 398166, Minneapolis, Minnesota 55439.
Copyright © 2019 by Abdo Consulting Group, Inc. International copyrights reserved in all countries.
No part of this book may be reproduced in any form without written permission from the publisher.
SportsZone™ is a trademark and logo of Abdo Publishing.

Printed in the United States of America, North Mankato, Minnesota
032018
092018

**THIS BOOK CONTAINS
RECYCLED MATERIALS**

Cover Photos: Kirsty Wigglesworth/AP Images, left; Robin Alam/Icon Sportswire/AP Images, right
Interior Photos: Bagu Blanco/Rex Features/AP Images, 4–5; Martin Mejia/AP Images, 6; Manu Fernandez/
AP Images, 9; Kieran McManus/Rex Features/AP Images, 10; Martin Rickett/PA Wire URN:9737819/
AP Images, 12–13; Lynne Cameron/Sportimage/Cal Sport Media/AP Images, 14; Phil Noble/PA Wire
URN:19356198/AP Images, 17; TGSPhoto/Rex Features/AP Images, 18–19; Martin Rickett/PA Wire
URN:22853665/AP Images, 20–21; Acero/Alter Photos/Sipa USA/AP Images, 23; Ruben Albarran/Rex
Features/AP Images, 24; Martin Meissner/AP Images, 27; Matt McNulty/Rex Features/AP Images, 28;
Lionel Urman/Sipa/AP Images, 30; Cameron Spencer/Getty Images Sport/Getty Images, 32–33; Fred
Kfoury III/Icon Sportswire/AP Images, 34; Bippa/AP Images, 36–37; Elaine Thompson/AP Images, 38–39;
Matt Dunham/AP Images, 40; Robin Alam/Icon Sportswire/AP Images, 42; Scott Winters/Icon Sportswire/
AP Images, 44–45; John Glanvill/AP Images, 45

Editor: Patrick Donnelly
Series Designer: Laura Polzin

Library of Congress Control Number: 2017962082

Publisher's Cataloging-in-Publication Data

Names: Avise, Jonathan, author.
Title: Great soccer debates / by Jonathan Avise.
Description: Minneapolis, Minnesota : Abdo Publishing, 2019. | Series: Great sports debates | Includes
    online resources and index.
Identifiers: ISBN 9781532114465 (lib.bdg.) | ISBN 9781532154294 (ebook)
Subjects: LCSH: Soccer players--Juvenile literature. | Soccer--Records--Juvenile literature. | Sports--
    History--Juvenile literature. | Debates and debating--Juvenile literature.
Classification: DDC 796.334--dc23

TABLE OF
CONTENTS

CHAPTER
ONE

MESSI OR RONALDO?

Ask just about anyone who the best soccer player in the world is and they'll likely come up with one of two names. Lionel Messi of Argentina and Portugal's Cristiano Ronaldo are the world's biggest soccer stars. They play for two of the world's biggest clubs—Messi for FC Barcelona and Ronaldo for Real Madrid. And from opposite sides of that heated Spanish rivalry, the high-scoring strikers have rewritten the record books.

They're not only great rivals on the field in Spain's La Liga. For nearly a decade, they've fought for the unofficial title of best player in the world. It's been an entertaining battle with no clear winner.

The two stars could not look or act more different. Ronaldo is tall, powerful, and graceful. He glides past opponents with great speed and delivers headers with power and accuracy. On the field he carries himself with the strut of a superstar. Off it, his smiling face is seen in advertisements throughout the world.

Messi, meanwhile, stands just 5 feet 7 inches tall. Short and quick, he has a knack for keeping possession in the tightest of spaces. The ball seems to never leave his foot. That allows Messi to dribble through forests of defenders and continue his attack on the net. And he lets his goals do the talking. Despite his monumental success, Messi most often shuns the spotlight.

Both players have developed into lethal scorers for their clubs as well as their countries. They battle each other for the honor of top scorer in La Liga. And both pour in goals for their teams in the prestigious Champions League.

Consistency has been a big part of both players' excellence. Starting with the 2009–10 season, Messi scored at least 40 goals for Barcelona in each of the next eight years. Ronaldo netted 50 or more goals for Real Madrid in six straight seasons beginning in 2010–11. No one else in world soccer has even approached the numbers posted by the amazing duo.

Ronaldo leaps high for a header during 2014 World Cup play.

Messi became Barcelona's all-time leading scorer in 2012 at just 24 years old. Through the 2016–17 season, just before he turned 30, Messi had scored 578 goals in 738 games for Barcelona and Argentina. He had also contributed 237 assists. Messi has been awarded the Ballon d'Or, given to the world's best player, five times.

Meanwhile, Ronaldo had scored 602 goals in 858 career games by the end of the 2016–17 season. His 600th career goal came in Real Madrid's 2017 Champions League Final blowout of Juventus. In 2016 he won his fourth Ballon d'Or. In that season alone he scored 55 goals, contributed 17 assists, and netted seven hat tricks in 57 games played.

Messi and Ronaldo haven't just racked up goals. Both have also helped their clubs win armfuls of trophies, too. Messi led Barcelona to the Spanish league title eight times through the end of the 2016–17 season. Real Madrid had won two La Liga championships with Ronaldo, including the 2016–17 title. Ronaldo also previously won three Premier League championships in England with Manchester United.

Both players have also been a part of teams that won the glamorous Champions League tournament, which includes

Messi's elite dribbling skills allow him to counter Ronaldo's size advantage.

WHO'S NEXT?

Brazilian star Neymar may be next in line to challenge for the title of best player in the world. The flashy forward starred first for Santos in his home country before moving on to play with Messi in Barcelona. Neymar signed with French giant Paris-Saint Germain in 2017. He has used his amazing dribbling skills, speed, and scoring ability to separate himself from the rest of the pack.

the best clubs from across Europe. Before Messi's arrival, Barcelona had won the European title just once. Since he debuted in 2005, the club has won four Champions League titles. Ronaldo won three European titles with Madrid, including back-to-back victories in 2016 and 2017. He also won a Champions League title with Manchester United in 2008.

Messi celebrates a goal against Juventus in 2017–18 Champions League action.

CHAPTER
TWO

HOW THE LEAGUES STACK UP

Without a doubt, England's Premier League is the most popular domestic league in the world. Millions of fans tune in to watch games each week from all over the globe. In the United States alone, an estimated 1.9 million viewers followed the action on the final day of the 2016–17 season.

Money and players from all soccer-playing continents have flooded into England since the league split off from the old English Football League in 1992. Star coaches and players populate teams up and down the lineup. However, while the

The clash between Manchester City (blue) and Manchester United (red) is typical of the fierce rivalries found in the Premier League.

Premier League is popular, is it the best in the world? At times Spain and Italy have argued their leagues are stronger. And Germany is home to some of Europe's biggest teams, too.

Some of the world's most famous soccer clubs compete in the Premier League. Many of them have more than a century of history on the pitch. Arsenal, Chelsea, Liverpool, Manchester United, and Tottenham Hotspur all have been playing for more than 100 years and have won numerous trophies.

Manchester City emerged as one of Europe's best clubs in the 2010s by signing some of the world's brightest stars. And even smaller English clubs such as Nottingham Forest and Aston Villa have won the European Cup in their history.

Premier League clubs aren't only about money and history, however. Its clubs also play a fast and physical style of soccer.

AMERICANS IN ENGLAND

American players have made their mark on one of the world's most exciting leagues. United States stars, such as Brian McBride (Fulham), Tim Howard (Manchester United, Everton), Brad Friedel (Liverpool, Blackburn Rovers, Aston Villa, Tottenham Hotspur), and Clint Dempsey (Fulham, Tottenham Hotspur), were important parts of their Premier League clubs during their time in England.

That makes for exciting and entertaining games for fans across the globe.

But for all that excitement, Premier League clubs haven't won many Champions League titles. Formerly called the European Cup, the tournament was renamed in 1992. In the next 25 years, Manchester United (1999 and 2008), Liverpool (2005), and Chelsea (2012) were the only English teams to win the European championship.

Meanwhile, clubs in Spain and Italy have been much more successful. Since 1992–93, Spanish giants Real Madrid (6 titles) and Barcelona (4) have combined to win 10 European titles, including four straight from 2014 to 2017. Italian clubs AC Milan (3), Internazionale, and Juventus have combined to capture five Champions League crowns. And Bayern Munich (2) and Borussia Dortmund have given Germany three European championships.

Despite the Premier League's relative lack of European success, soccer's biggest names still arrive each season on England's shores. Legendary players from throughout Europe have made their names in the Premier League. Paul Pogba and Thierry Henry of France, Mesut Özil and Jürgen Klinsmann of

Germany, and Spain's Fernando Torres and David Silva all found another level of stardom in England.

And the Premier League teams' big budgets allow that trend to continue. In 2017 international stars Spaniard Álvaro Morata and Brazilian Gabriel Jesus landed huge contracts with Chelsea and Manchester City, respectively. That's in addition to English stars, such as Tottenham's Harry Kane and Marcus Rashford

Manchester United celebrates its Champions League title in 1999.

Harry Kane's scoring talents put Tottenham Hotspur among the elite clubs in the Premier League.

of Manchester United, who make headlines with their own standout performances.

Germany's Bundesliga, Spain's La Liga, and Italy's Serie A can revel in their big clubs, such as Bayern Munich, Real Madrid,

and Juventus. Those clubs have won more European trophies than their English rivals. But for excitement and star power, it's hard to top the English Premier League.

David Beckham became one of the biggest stars in the world while playing for Manchester United in the late 1990s and early 2000s.

CHAPTER
THREE

SUPERCLUBS

Soccer is different from major American sports. Many countries have their own leagues, and each has its own stories of legendary players and teams. Each league has its dominant clubs, teams similar to baseball's New York Yankees or American football's New England Patriots, that seem to have all the success and all the riches.

So which of the big clubs can claim to be the biggest? Certainly the richest and most successful teams historically have come from Europe.

MANCHESTER UNITED

Thanks to players such as David Beckham, Eric Cantona, Wayne Rooney, and Paul Pogba, Manchester United has never been short of star power in its famous red shirts. The club has been the most successful team in England's Premier League era, which began in 1992. Manchester United has won 20 league titles in its history, including 13 in the first 25 years of Premier League play. Add to that three European titles and 12 FA Cups and it's easy to make the argument that the club is the most successful in English history.

All that winning has helped Manchester United become one of the most powerful soccer clubs ever. It was ranked as the richest club in the world in 2017. That helps the team continue to bring in new stars such as Romelu Lukaku and Anthony Martial to replace aging players and bolster an already impressive lineup.

REAL MADRID

No club has won more on Europe's biggest stage than Real Madrid. On a warm night in Cardiff, Wales, a pair of goals from superstar Cristiano Ronaldo helped Madrid win the

Karim Benzema, *left*, and Gareth Bale celebrate a Real Madrid goal in 2017.

2017 Champions League final. The 4–1 victory over Juventus marked the second consecutive Champions League title for the giants of Spain. That would be an enormous feat for most soccer clubs. For Madrid, in a way, it was just more of the same.

Nicknamed Los Blancos for their all-white kits, Real Madrid has been a dominant presence in European soccer since

the 1950s. The club won the first five European Cups, the tournament that became the Champions League. The 2017 title was No. 12 overall, giving Los Blancos five more than the next closest team, AC Milan of Italy.

Many of the world's biggest names have called Madrid home over the years. In addition to the Portuguese legend Ronaldo, other international stars such as Alfredo di Stefano from Argentina, Zinedine Zidane of France, Brazilian Ronaldo, and Gareth Bale from Wales all found success in the Spanish capital city.

BARCELONA

To FC Barcelona supporters the team is *més que un club*—that is, "more than a club." The famous blue-and-garnet shirts of Barcelona represent a huge fan base in the Spanish region of Catalonia and around the world. Like its archrival in Madrid, Barcelona is a force in Spain's La Liga. And they've become a major player in the Champions League, too.

Lionel Messi, *left*, and Andrés Iniesta pose with the winners' trophy after FC Barcelona defeated Alavés in the 2017 Copa del Rey final.

For a long time, Barcelona chased Real Madrid's European triumphs. In recent years the gap has closed. A slew of league titles—24 through 2017—and five European championships make Barcelona one of the most successful teams in history. And an incredible roster of players past and present has made them one of the most beautiful clubs to watch.

Lionel Messi has scored goal after goal for Barcelona. And the roster of past greats is almost too long to believe. Legends Johan Cruyff, Xavi, Ronaldinho, and Rivaldo are among the world's best players who have called Barcelona home over the years.

BAYERN MUNICH

In Germany, no club is bigger than the Bavarian behemoth, Bayern Munich. The team in red and white from southern Germany has dominated the Bundesliga. Its résumé includes 27 league championships and 18 German Cups through 2017. Bayern's five European titles rank third-best all time, providing further evidence of its place among the world's biggest clubs.

Bayern Munich's Robert Lewandowski falls to the ground but beats
Dortmund keeper Roman Buerki in a 2017 Bundesliga match.

Bayern has been a magnet for legendary German players. Their roster of past greats include some of the best players to ever take the field.

"The Kaiser" Franz Beckenbauer, "The Bomber" Gerd Müller, Karl-Heinz Rummenigge, Jürgen Klinsmann, and Michael Ballack all represented Bayern Munich. Recent stars, such as Germany's Thomas Müller and Manuel Neuer and Robert Lewandowski of Poland, have kept the club among the best in Europe.

A roster loaded with talented stars from around the world has put Manchester City among the world's elite clubs.

AC MILAN

Another of the biggest in the world is Italy's AC Milan. The club hit hard times after getting caught up in a match-fixing scandal in 2006. Since then, success in the Italian league has been hard to come by. But Milan has collected lots of hardware in its history. The club's seven European titles trail only Real Madrid.

NEW KIDS ON THE BLOCK

Does a soccer club need cases full of trophies or heaps of history to be the world's biggest team? Two European teams with more riches than trophies would argue no.

Manchester City and Paris Saint-Germain have made meteoric rises in the 2010s. Both clubs were purchased by super-wealthy owners who have invested heavily in some of the world's best players. Both are determined to prove they are the best of the best.

Manchester City, known as the Citizens, won the Premier League titles in 2011–12 and 2013–14 and is now a regular participant in the Champions League. Its lineup includes some of the best players in the world. Sergio Aguero, David Silva, and Kevin De Bruyne have helped make the Citizens, with their striking sky-blue jerseys, a dominant force in England.

Paris Saint-Germain, or PSG, has lapped the field in France's Ligue 1. The club won four consecutive league titles from 2013 to 2016 and has been home to some of the most exciting players in the world. Zlatan Ibrahimovic, Angel Di Maria, and Edinson Cavani have all called Paris home in that time.

Champions League glory, however, still eluded PSG. So in the summer of 2017, the team made its biggest splash yet. The club purchased Brazilian superstar Neymar from Barcelona for a record $263 million. By spending big money, the club's owners believed they had done enough to capture their first Champions League title.

Paris Saint-Germain made headlines when it signed Neymar, *right*, away from FC Barcelona in 2017.

Manuel Neuer can't stop Frank Lampard's shot in the 2010 World Cup, but without replay technology the apparent goal was disallowed.

CHAPTER
FOUR

VIDEO: YES OR NO?

It was the first half of a 2010 World Cup knockout game in South Africa. England trailed Germany 2–1. England's Frank Lampard gathered a loose ball and lofted a powerful shot toward the German goal. The ball looped over German goalkeeper Manuel Neuer, cracked against the crossbar, and landed just over the goal line. England had tied its rival 2–2.

Or at least it *should* have drawn England level in the Round of 16 matchup. But the referee ruled the ball hadn't gone in and allowed play to continue. England's players were furious. And soon they were behind even further on the way to a shocking 4–1 loss.

Many leagues and competitions around the globe now use goal-line technology to avoid refereeing mistakes such as that disallowed goal. Cameras and assistant referees help officials make the correct calls. World soccer's governing body, the Fédération Internationale de Football Association (FIFA), used the technology for the first time at the 2014 World Cup in Brazil.

Now, some leagues want to go further. Some are introducing video assistant referees to review other parts of the game: offside calls, penalties, and potential red-card offenses.

Major League Soccer (MLS) in the United States started using replay in 2017. Germany's Bundesliga began its use, too. And the 2018 World Cup in Russia was scheduled to be the first major international tournament to use it during games. That decision marked an enormous change at the world's biggest sporting event.

Supporters of video assistant referees, called VAR, say it's an easy call. Video replay will mean fewer mistakes. Supporters also hope it will mean fewer scenes of angry players crowded around a referee to plead their case.

A referee uses replay to confirm a goal during an MLS match in 2017.

West Germany keeper Hans Tilkowski watches Geoff Hurst's controversial game-winning goal in the 1966 World Cup final.

Detractors, however, say replay will slow the game. Players and fans in the stands can be left confused when an exciting play goes to review. And unlike other sports that use

GEOFF HURST'S GOAL

Goal-line technology or video replay could have helped clear up one of soccer's most controversial goals. England and West Germany were deadlocked in extra time of the 1966 World Cup final in London. England's Geoff Hurst unleashed a shot that hit the crossbar and landed just over the goal line. Or did it? The goal was awarded. England won the World Cup. But German fans have long argued that Hurst's famous goal shouldn't have counted.

instant replay, many calls in soccer are open to a referee's interpretation. Did that player *mean* to elbow his opponent? What's shown on video may not determine the player's intent, which a referee should be in a better position to interpret.

Modern technology has finally arrived in the world's game. Whether that's a positive development is up for review.

CHAPTER
FIVE

AMERICAN DREAMS

The United States has the upper hand over the rest of the
world in many sports. In basketball, gridiron football,
baseball, and other activities, Americans are considered
the best.

But in the world's most popular sport, the United States
is most often an afterthought. The US Men's National Team
(USMNT) qualified for seven straight World Cups between
1990 and 2014. But the team never came close to winning the
tournament. Can it go all the way?

The US Women's National Team (USWNT) has won three
FIFA Women's World Cups. It helped that the United States got
a head start on many countries. Girls and women were given

greater opportunity to participate in sports in the United States with the passage of Title IX legislation in 1972. That led to early development of women's soccer in the United States, while other countries focused only on their men's teams. The rest of the world has begun to catch up to the Americans, but the USWNT is still the predominant power in women's soccer.

The USMNT poses before its 2014 World Cup game against Belgium.

ONE GREAT RUN

The USMNT's best run at a World Cup found the team on the verge of a shocking berth in the semifinals. In the 2002 tournament in South Korea and Japan, the United States stunned the world. First the Americans upset Portugal in the group stage before knocking out continental rival Mexico in the Round of 16. They then very nearly pulled the biggest surprise of all in the quarterfinals. But the Americans lost to eventual runner-up Germany 1–0.

On the other hand, American men have been playing catch-up with the rest of the world. The United States neglected the sport for decades in the 20th century as its popularity exploded in other countries. The United States did not qualify for the World Cup between 1950 and 1990. But the American men have slowly begun to have international success.

First the nation qualified for the 1990 World Cup. Then the United States hosted the 1994 tournament. That gave the sport a boost on US soil by drawing the interest of millions of new fans. Trips to the knockout stages at the 2002, 2010, and 2014 tournaments have helped advance the American game. And the growth of MLS in the United States has given more American players a chance to play professionally. MLS began in 1996 and now has teams across the United States and Canada.

Other factors could be holding US men's soccer back. Most countries across the globe attract their very best athletes to the soccer field. In the United States, soccer has to compete with more popular sports for the attention of its young athletes. America has produced many talented professional soccer players, such as Eric Wynalda, Brian McBride, Landon Donovan, and Clint Dempsey. But what if the best players from other American sports had turned to soccer early on instead?

The United States does have a young star who is already making waves at one of the biggest clubs in Europe. Christian Pulisic, only 19 years old at the start of the 2017–18 season, quickly became one of the best players in the German Bundesliga for Borussia Dortmund. Could Pulisic be the star to help bring the USMNT to the next level? A disappointing showing in World Cup qualifying kept the United States on the sideline for the 2018 tournament. But US soccer fans hope that missing the World Cup will become a rare event going forward.

Even the play of rising star Christian Pulisic couldn't help the United States qualify for the 2018 World Cup.

TOPICS FOR FURTHER
DISCUSSION

- Who's the best American player of all time?

- Should FIFA expand the World Cup?

- Who is the best manager ever?

- Which is the best national team not to win the World Cup—1974 Holland or 1982 Brazil?

- Is promotion/relegation right for US soccer?

- Will MLS ever be one of the best leagues in the world?

- Which is the best team of all time?

- **Pelé or Maradona—who was better?**

GLOSSARY

CLUB
The team a player competes with outside of his or her national team.

DOMESTIC LEAGUE
A league made up of teams from a particular country—e.g., England's Premier League, Spain's La Liga, Germany's Bundesliga.

DRIBBLE
The touches on the ball by a player as it is taken up the field.

HAT TRICK
Three goals by the same player in one game.

HEADER
Striking the ball with one's head.

KNOCKOUT
The stage of a soccer tournament when one loss eliminates a team.

OFFSIDE
An infraction that is called when a player is closer to the goal than the last defender (other than the keeper) when the ball is kicked.

PROMOTION
A team moving up from a lower level of competition to a stronger league.

RELEGATION
Demoting a team from a higher league to a lower league.

ROUND OF 16
The round of a tournament that begins with 16 teams left; usually the first round of knockout games that takes place after group play.

STRIKER
A forward position in soccer tasked with scoring goals.

ONLINE
RESOURCES

Booklinks
NONFICTION NETWORK
FREE! ONLINE NONFICTION RESOURCES

To learn more about great soccer debates, visit **abdobooklinks.com**. These links are routinely monitored and updated to provide the most current information available.

MORE
INFORMATION

BOOKS

Gifford, Clive, and John Malam. *The Complete Book of Soccer*. Buffalo, NY: Firefly Books Ltd., 2016.

Jökulsson, Illugi. *USA Men's Team: New Stars on the Field*. New York: Abbeville Press Publishers, 2014.

Kortemeier, Todd. *Total Soccer*. Minneapolis, MN: Abdo Publishing, 2017.

INDEX

ABOUT THE AUTHOR

Jonathan Avise is a reporter, writer, and digital media editor from Minneapolis, Minnesota. An avid soccer fan, he is a die-hard supporter of North London's Tottenham Hotspur.